FOREWORD

The Army and the nation are entering a period of significant change, which includes a transition from conflict to sustainment in an uncertain and contentious world, a strategic focus pivot from the Middle East and Europe to the Asia-Pacific region, and a resourcing environment shift from one of plenty to one of fiscal austerity. We will adapt to these changing conditions as we effectively execute the **RDECOM mission to empower, unburden, protect, and sustain the Soldier through integrated research, development, and engineering solutions.**

Shortly after I became Director in 2012, and in the absence of a clear strategy, the Command leadership team issued the RDECOM Campaign Plan (FY13–14) to give the Command a near-term direction with specific goals while we took the time needed to craft a new strategic direction. This document, *Maximizing Land Combat Power*, describes the RDECOM strategy for adapting to the challenges of our current environment while continuing to provide world-class science and engineering solutions to our Soldiers. It identifies those core competencies required to support the Army's enduring needs as well as those areas of increasing emphasis and priority to ensure our Soldiers are prepared for the future fight. Our research, technology, and engineering portfolios will remain responsive to our Army leadership's strategic goals and objectives, as well as to the threats and challenges facing our Soldiers. In addition, we will continue to tie together our Science and Technology (S&T) work with our engineering expertise through our Prototype Integration Facilities (PIFs) to reduce the cost-and-schedule uncertainty as well as the technology risk in our acquisition programs. This strategy also includes a description of several grand challenges, or Director's Initiatives, which will draw upon competencies from across the Command to develop and demonstrate innovative concepts that will provide leap-ahead capabilities for Soldiers of the future. Over the next six to eight months, we will revise our RDECOM Campaign Plan FY15 and beyond to describe the specific goals and objectives required to execute this strategy.

This document is aligned with the Army Campaign Plan and the Army Materiel Command (AMC) Strategic Plan 2013–2023 and serves to communicate our future strategic direction to implement the **RDECOM vision as the Army's go-to organization for superior scientific and engineering expertise that defines the space between the state of the art and the art of the possible and ensures global dominance across the range of military operations** to Army leadership, stakeholders, customers, partners, and our internal workforce.

ARMY STRONG

Dale A. Ormond
Director

TABLE OF CONTENTS

EMPOWER, UNBURDEN, PROTECT, AND SUSTAIN THE SOLDIER

The U.S. Army Research Development and Engineering Command (RDECOM) is the largest single provider of research, technology development, engineering, and systems analysis for the Army. Under the command and leadership of AMC, and in support of the Assistant Secretary of the Army for Acquisition, Logistics and Technology (ASA(ALT)), RDECOM executes the mission to empower, unburden, protect, and sustain the Soldier through integrated research, development, and engineering solutions. Aligned with the AMC Strategic Plan 2013–2023, RDECOM is responsible for all materiel-related technology and engineering in support of generating Army Land Combat Power. RDECOM provides technology integration across all aspects of Land Combat Power development; provides unbiased technical advice and expertise to the Training and Doctrine Command (TRADOC), Program Executive Officers/Program Managers (PEOs/PMs), and industry; and collaborates across the larger Army Research and Development (R&D) community: with the Corps of Engineers' Engineer Research and Development Center (ERDC), Medical Research and Materiel Command (MRMC), Army Research Institute (ARI), Space and Missile Defense Command (SMDC), University Affiliated Research Centers (UARCs), Federally Funded Research and Development Centers (FFRDCs), the Defense Advanced Research Projects Agency

> **Mission:** Empower, unburden, protect, and sustain the Soldier through integrated research, development, and engineering solutions.

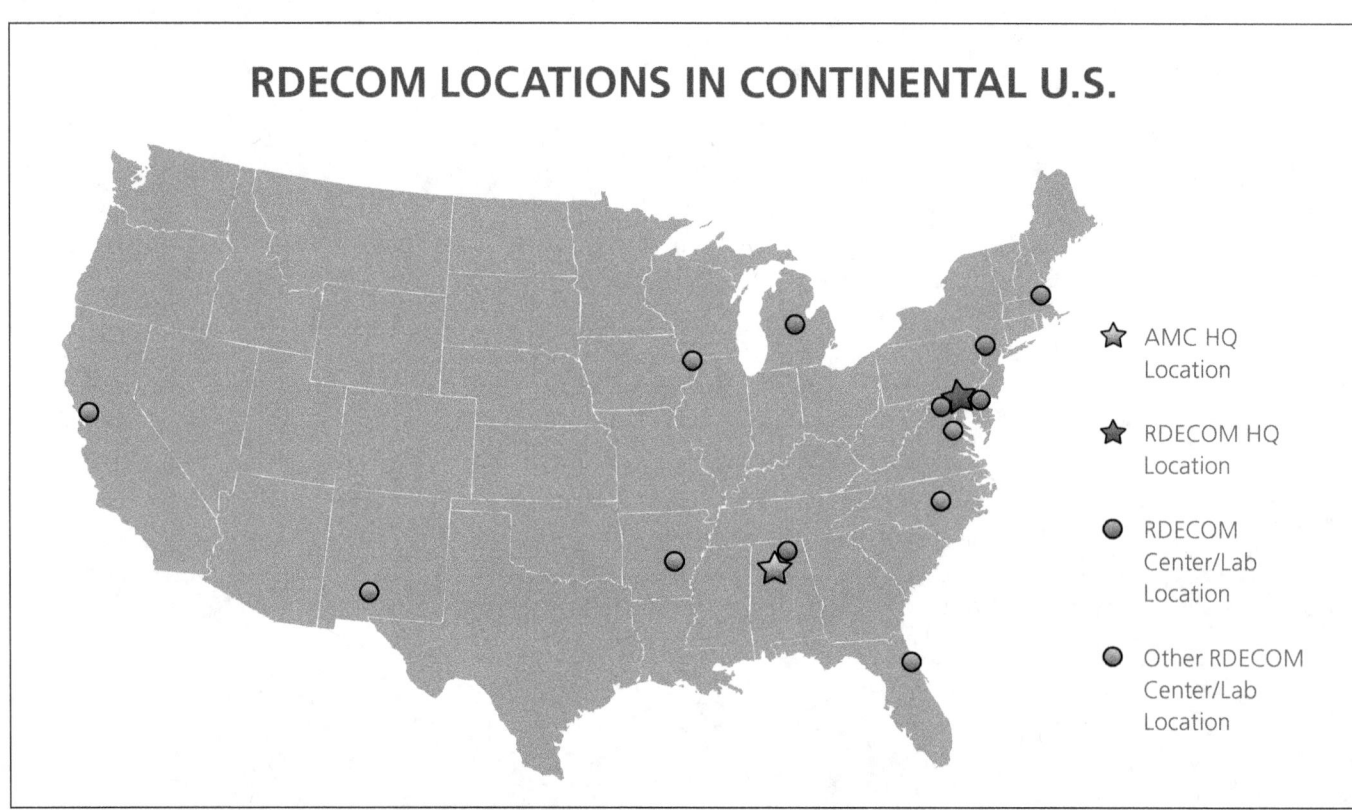

RDECOM LOCATIONS IN CONTINENTAL U.S.

☆ AMC HQ Location

★ RDECOM HQ Location

● RDECOM Center/Lab Location

● Other RDECOM Center/Lab Location

EMPOWER, UNBURDEN, PROTECT, AND SUSTAIN THE SOLDIER (CONT)

(DARPA), sister services, other government organizations, industry, and academia. As the leader for research and development of Army materiel, RDECOM drives the nation's science and technology agenda for the Army. As the provider of life cycle engineering expertise, RDECOM serves as the nation's systems engineering leader for Land Combat Power.

Through the largest concentration of scientists and engineers in the Army, RDECOM conducts research to generate revolutionary capabilities designed to make current systems obsolete; discovers, develops, and demonstrates high-payoff technologies needed to mitigate emerging threats; and provides affordable enhanced capabilities to extend the life and reduce the operation and maintenance costs of existing systems. RDECOM comprises the Army Research Laboratory (ARL) and the Army's Research Development and Engineering Centers (RDECs) organized as shown in Appendix A, with facilities strategically co-located to support AMC's Life Cycle Management Commands (LCMCs) and the PEOs. Recognized for its leadership in innovation, scientific discovery, capability development, and the transition of materiel solutions, RDECOM workforce accomplishments include many national and international awards, numerous patents, an extensive portfolio of publications in peer-reviewed journals, and the majority of Army's greatest invention awards, many of which are credited with saving Soldiers' lives.

Vision: RDECOM is the Army's go-to organization for superior scientific and engineering expertise that defines the space between the state of the art and the art of the possible and ensures global dominance.

CHALLENGES OF A CHANGING STRATEGIC ENVIRONMENT

The current strategic environment is creating a major shift in the challenges and opportunities that directly affect RDECOM's role as the Army's provider of technology and engineering support for Land Combat Power. The strategic trends affecting RDECOM include the transition from conflict to sustainment, the pivot to the Asia-Pacific region, and the emerging fiscal austerity facing defense. RDECOM's efforts to address these priorities will support, leverage, and amplify AMC's strategic Lines of Effort in alignment with the Army Campaign Plan 2012 Army end state.

The transition from conflict to sustainment has historically signaled a period of declining resources. After more than a decade of conflict, during which delivering capability to the Soldier as soon as possible was the priority, the bow wave of cost to sustain these systems makes it an imperative to re-architect our systems to reduce the sustainment costs and facilitate future capabilities growth. The shift to Asia-Pacific, while maintaining all commitments to partners throughout Europe and the Middle East, is expected to create fluidity and unpredictability in the landscape of emerging threats to U.S. national interests. Per the National Defense Strategic Guidance, the future defense threat environment is described as volatile, uncertain, complex, and ambiguous with numerous groups hostile to U.S. intentions having access to near-peer technologies, especially in the areas of computer networks, biotechnology, anti-access and area denial, and information

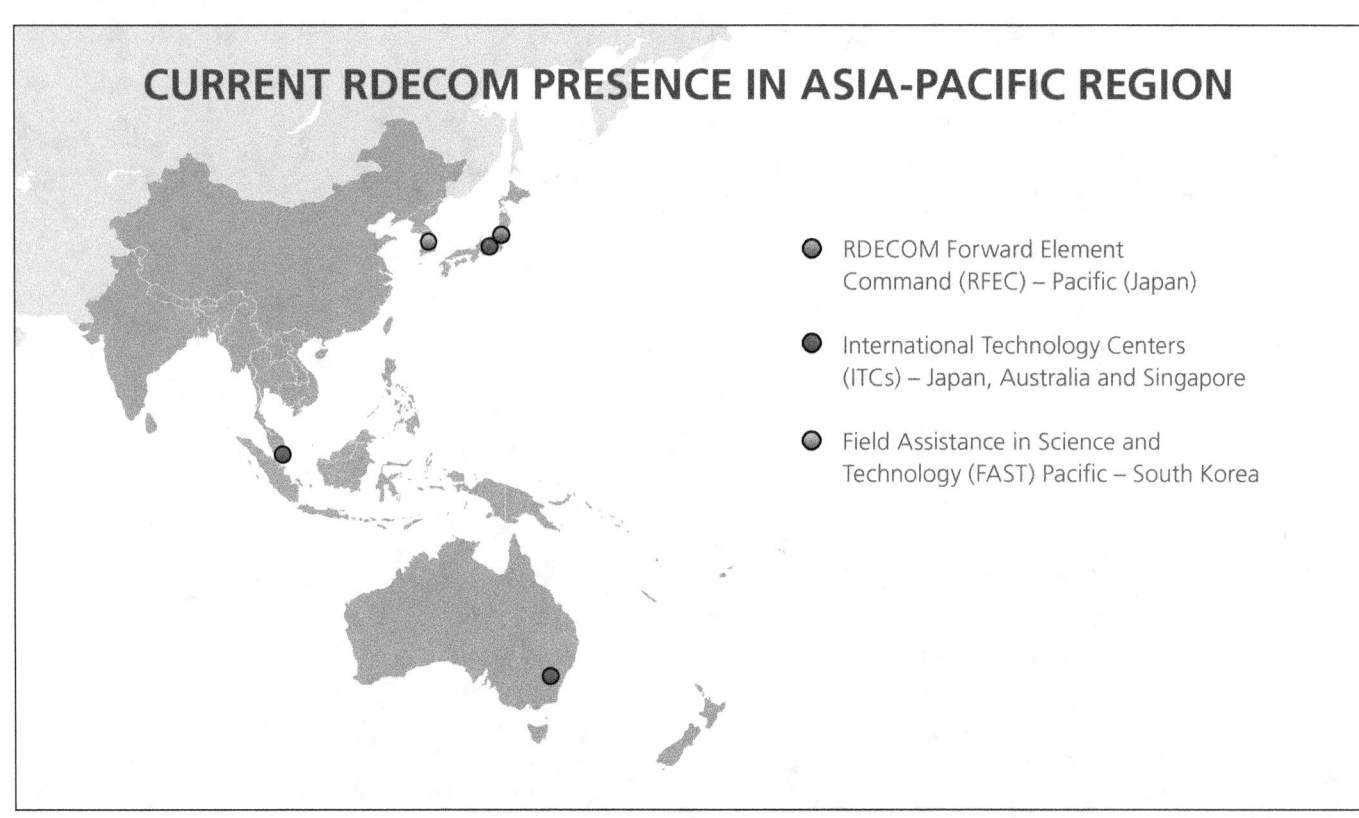

CURRENT RDECOM PRESENCE IN ASIA-PACIFIC REGION

- ● RDECOM Forward Element Command (RFEC) – Pacific (Japan)
- ● International Technology Centers (ITCs) – Japan, Australia and Singapore
- ● Field Assistance in Science and Technology (FAST) Pacific – South Korea

technology. This environment will drive RDECOM's science and technology priorities in new directions to both prevent and create technological surprise, and to counter emerging threats, while still maintaining focus on the enduring needs of the Army. Bounded by the realities of fiscal austerity, RDECOM will develop innovative technologies to change the nature of the fight; leverage commercial developments where possible to address emerging threats; and improve the operational effectiveness, affordability, sustainability, and interoperability of legacy systems.

The current fiscal environment is likely to result in fielding fewer new systems with a corresponding need to extend the lifetime of legacy systems. Therefore, RDECOM will focus on maintaining and creating technologies to enable incremental capability upgrades, reduce sustainment costs, and extend capability life. With the continually changing threats over the last twelve years, RDECOM had a significant near-term effort to support our Soldiers in the midst of a fight. The cessation of direct action enables RDECOM to change our science and technology investment priorities to discover, develop, mature, and demonstrate technologies that provide enhanced capabilities for the next generation of Army systems. Within this environment, RDECOM's strategy and priorities for the future are shaped by guidance and direction from the Office of the Secretary of Defense (OSD),

> **RDECOM will invest in areas of Army needs which are not adequately served by the private sector, while maintaining technical proficiency in enduring core competencies for the Army.**

Army leadership, ASA(ALT), AMC, Special Operations Forces (SOF), PEO customers, and TRADOC. RDECOM, with the other services, academia, other government agencies, industry, and the PEOs, helped define Army long-range investment strategies as captured in the 30-year capability roadmaps. This long-term investment strategy is consistent with ASA(ALT)'s Top Challenges and TRADOC's Science and Technology Investment Areas as shown in Appendix B.

The current global and national fiscal environment will force decisions relating to Army structure, readiness, and equipment modernization. To this end, RDECOM will continue to invest in areas primarily driven by the Army's needs where commercial investments are minimal, while maintaining proficiency but reduced investments in areas where technology requirements are either no longer top priorities or technology development is adequately covered in the private sector, academia, other services, or other government agencies. As budget pressures mount, deliberate investment in S&T will emphasize areas that address Army-unique challenges and necessitate greater collaboration with others within the Army S&T Enterprise, our sister services, the FFRDCs, academia, industry, and international partners to solve common challenges.

CORE COMPETENCIES OF THE ARMY'S TECHNOLOGY SPECTRUM

The Army depends on RDECOM to execute an integrated program portfolio that is responsive to the highest priorities as defined by our stakeholders and customers. An analysis of TRADOC Warfighter Outcomes reveals that capabilities required for the future not only depend on our core technical competencies, but that the vast majority of needed capabilities require systems engineering solutions across multiple competencies to anticipate and exploit emerging technologies that will deliver capabilities to the Soldier. The breadth and depth of our core competencies and systems engineering expertise is a unique national asset. RDECOM's core competencies, shown in the text box on page 6 and further developed in Appendix C, cover the broad range of technologies needed to address the Army's capabilities across the range of military operations. RDECOM's scientists and engineers have a deep understanding of technology and the state of the art, of the threat environment in which the technology must operate, and, most importantly, the missions our Soldiers must execute. In this way, RDECOM provides expert technical advice and analysis to inform TRADOC requirements, evaluates emerging technologies and their potential impact on the fight, and supports the acquisition community by enabling a smart-buyer paradigm. RDECOM's ability to span the research, development, and engineering spectrum; integrate across the broad range of core technical competencies; and translate technological innovations into Army capabilities enables RDECOM to push the state of the art and realize the art of the possible for the Army.

RDECOM's core competencies depend upon a preeminent, multi-disciplinary, adaptive workforce that conducts leading-edge research, development, and life cycle engineering, while promoting discovery and innovation

CORE COMPETENCIES OF THE ARMY'S TECHNOLOGY SPECTRUM (CONT)

across government, academia and industry. To execute the AMC Strategic Plan Line of Effort (LOE) #4, RDECOM must:

- Recruit, develop, and retain a highly capable workforce with expertise in the critical core competencies necessary to support Army technological needs now and in the future;

- Aggressively develop the next generation workforce through Science, Technology, Engineering, and Mathematics outreach, student internships, the military officer scientist program, the U.S. Military Academy faculty exchange program, National Research Council post-doctoral fellows, and employee mentoring, training, and development programs; and

- Maintain state-of-the-art technical infrastructure to support our mission, recognizing that infrastructure, as with intellectual capital, must continuously adapt to enable technological advancements.

RDECOM will utilize authorities provided through legislation, such as Section 219, to invest in our people, equipment, and infrastructure to support our Soldiers and continually advance the state of the art.

RDECOM invests hundreds of millions of dollars each year in academia and industry worldwide. The academic engagement is executed through a robust single investigator research program, as well as other mechanisms such as Centers of Excellence, Cooperative Technology Alliances (CTAs),

RDECOM Core Competencies

Soldier Systems

Aviation Systems

C4ISR Technologies

Chemical and Biological Defense

Ground Vehicles

Missiles and Rocket Systems

Weapons and Munitions

Life Cycle Systems Engineering

Fundamental Research

Multidisciplinary University Research Initiatives (MURIs), UARCs, and presentations at, and participation in, technology and scientific conferences. RDECOM engages with industry through a variety of mechanisms, including Collaborative Research and Development Agreements (CRADAs), the Small Business Innovative Research Program (SBIR), and industry-funded research and development efforts. RDECOM entered into more than 100 new CRADAs with industry and academia in 2012, and we will continue to nurture these collaborations and partnerships as an effective force multiplier for our core technical competencies. Through our leadership and support of global research and development, RDECOM effectively shapes the nation's science and technology agenda in support of Army requirements.

RDECOM covers the globe seeking opportunities to leverage the latest innovations in science and technology through RDECOM Forward Element Commands (RFECs) located in the Atlantic, Pacific, and Americas. Our International Technology Centers (ITCs) and the Field Assistance in Science and Technology (FAST) advisors constitute the regionally located RFECs. ITCs promote international partnership through the development of S&T collaborations with foreign universities, industry, and governments to obtain the most advanced state-of-the-art technology. RDECOM supports operational Army requirements through a network of embedded FAST science advisors. These FAST science advisors identify real-time capability needs and long-term strategic science and technology focus areas from the Combatant Commands, Army Operating Forces, and Combat Training Centers. The capability needs are sent to RDECOM for analysis and rapid identification of solutions. Each RFEC has a prioritized list of engagement strategies with our international partners' academia, industries, and militaries to develop partnerships and collaborative agreements in concert with strategic goals of ASA(ALT) and TRADOC. These engagements, in support of Combatant Commander regional objectives, help to develop and strengthen our military-to-military ties with current and potential international partners. RFEC efforts are critical to ensuring that the Army stays current with the latest developments in state-of-the-art technologies developed around the globe.

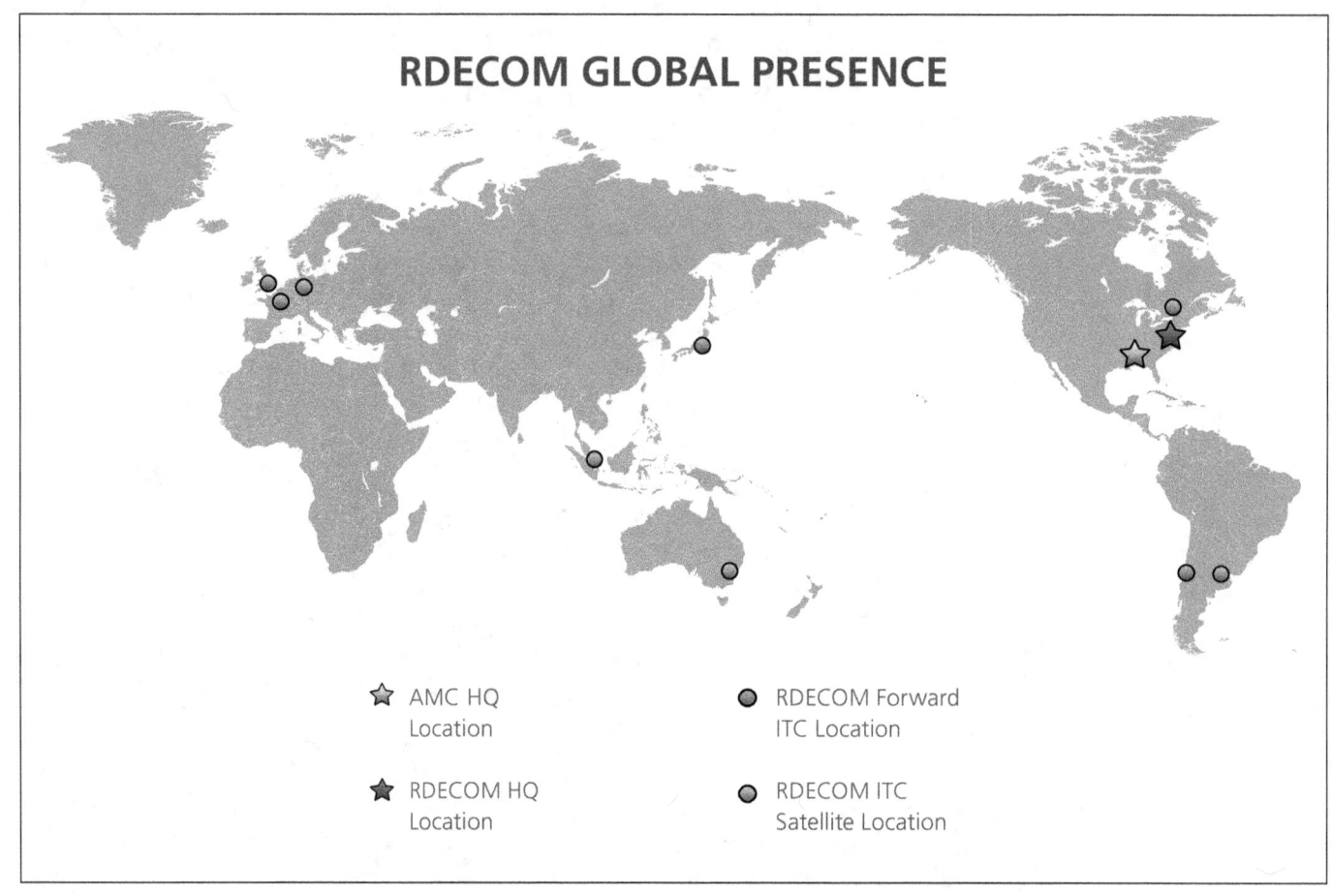

RDECOM GLOBAL PRESENCE

☆ AMC HQ Location

★ RDECOM HQ Location

⬤ RDECOM Forward ITC Location

⬤ RDECOM ITC Satellite Location

RESEARCH: SEEDS OF DISCOVERY AND INNOVATION

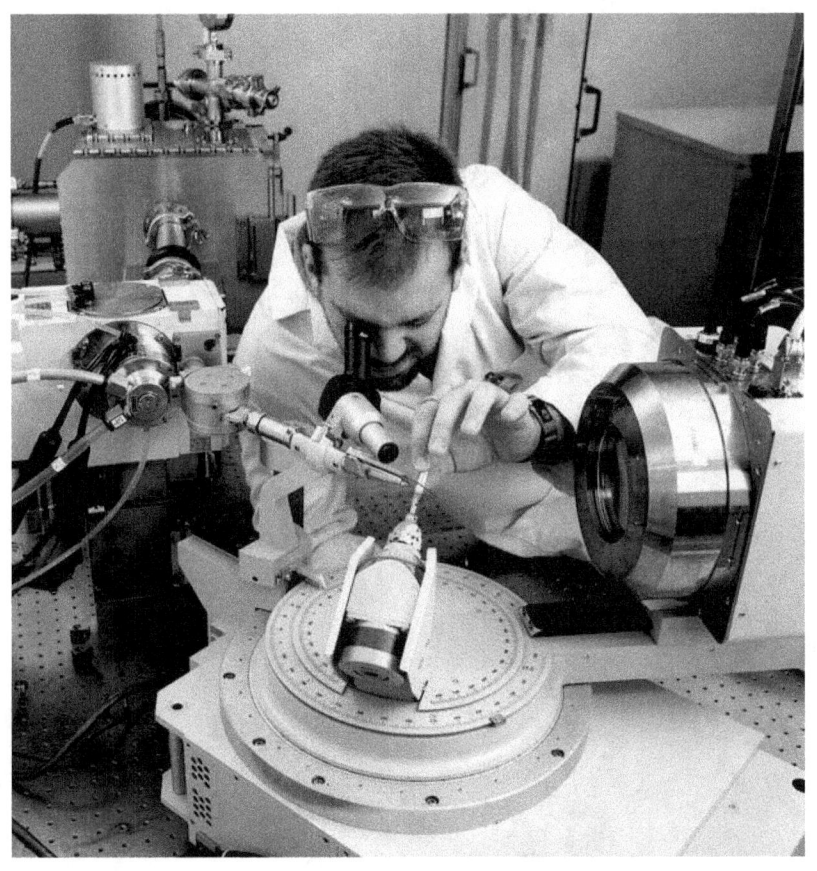

RDECOM executes a broad-based program of fundamental research that generates and transforms leading-edge scientific discoveries into new technologies with substantial military potential. We conduct research with academia, other Army S&T organizations, sister services, other government laboratories, industry, and international partners. RDECOM not only executes in-house research and leverages research and technology efforts from our partners, but also drives the nation's

> RDECOM drives the nation's science and technology agenda through its leadership and collaboration with an extensive network of private-sector science and technology performers.

science and technology agenda through our leadership of, and influence in, an extensive network of private-sector science and technology performers. RDECOM has identified a number of strategic research areas within our portfolio for additional emphasis. These are based on the AMC Commanding General's priorities as outlined in LOE #3 for their potential to provide game-changing capabilities for Soldiers of the future and essentially make current capabilities obsolete. These include:

Quantum information sciences: conduct fundamental research and investigation of deep properties of quantum mechanics, such as entanglement and superposition, and their consequences, which can lead to revolutionary capabilities beyond the limits of classical physics in information processing, sensing, communications, and imaging.

Materials in extreme environments: develop a fundamental understanding of, and an ability to model and design materials across, a wide range of scales (e.g., atomistic, nano, micro, continuum) to ultimately provide material technologies that enable next-generation multifunctional performance in integrated protection, lethality, electronics, and power and energy concepts that drastically reduce weight while enhancing capability over a range of operational and threat environments.

Network science: derive the fundamental laws of the evolution and behaviors of living and constructed networks, treating them as holistic organisms to enable revolutionary advances in the ability to model, design, analyze, predict, and control the joint behavior of secure communications, sensing, and command-and-control networks.

Advanced computing: focus on ways to harness an ever-growing set of computers, from use of large-scale supercomputers to hand-held devices, to ultimately put the power of supercomputing in the hands of the Soldier for better control of the operational space.

Human sciences: focus on gaining a fundamental understanding of Soldier performance, to include study of human neurocognitive processes, neurally based monitoring of health and functional states, and intelligent Soldier-system interactions.

Extreme energy science: provide dense component technologies from the nano to the micro scales that provide efficient energy production, storage, and use to enhance Soldier mobility, survivability, and lethality while reducing the logistical burden.

Intelligent systems: conduct research in perception, intelligence, mobility, manipulation, and human systems integration to enable a range of air and ground robotic platforms to empower and unburden Soldiers in complex terrain.

Cybernetics: assimilate the learning, cognition, adaptation, social control, communication, and connectivity that will enable efficient and effective control and cooperation between humans and machines.

Synthetic molecular systems: use the tools of synthetic biology to design materials and manufacturing processes that are not found in nature and are difficult or impossible to replicate via traditional chemical or physical processes.

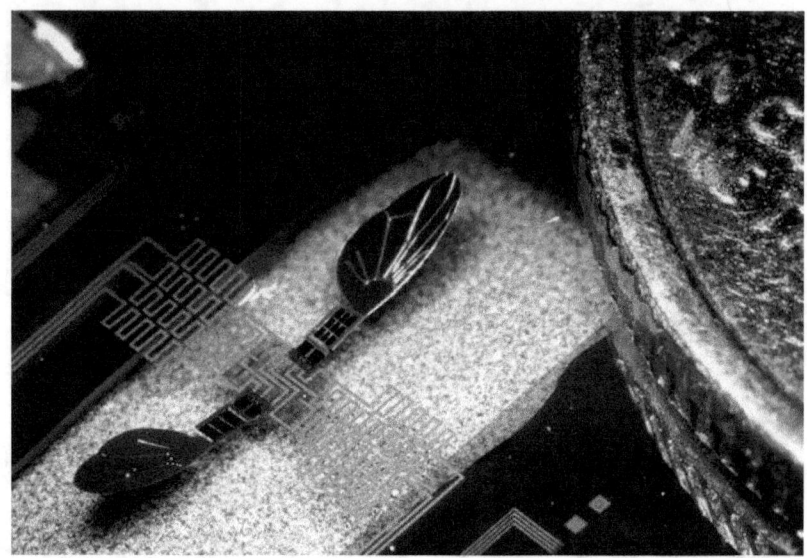

Nanotechnology: conduct research into materials designed at nano-scales, which have properties radically different from the same materials at meso- or macro-scales, and can be exploited for energy generation and storage, armor, adaptive signature management, and a host of other military applications.

TECHNOLOGY DEVELOPMENT: USER REQUIREMENTS TO COUNTER ENDURING AND EMERGING THREATS

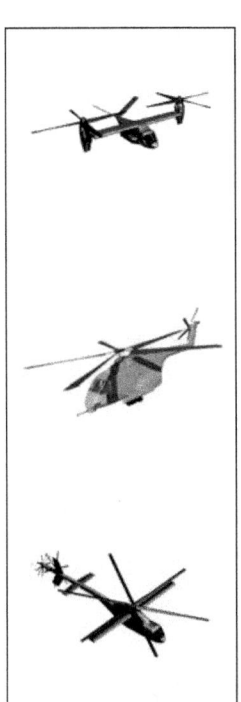

RDECOM engages TRADOC, the intelligence community, Combatant Commanders, and PEOs to understand emerging threats and the operational requirements that next-generation systems will face. Our scientists and engineers interact with their peers across the science and technology community to maintain awareness of science and technology trends and opportunities. These interactions allow RDECOM to develop and execute a cutting-edge technology portfolio informed by the highest priority needs of our stakeholders in response to both current and projected future operational environments. Within this portfolio, a number of areas have been identified for additional emphasis based on AMC Commanding General's priorities, the AMC Strategic Plan 2013–2023 (LOE #3), TRADOC's highest priorities, and ASA(ALT)'s Top Challenges:

Joint multi-role aircraft: pursue a number of new technologies to address the challenges presented by the fact that the current vertical lift capability lacks sufficient speed, endurance, and lift to perform a number of critical missions in the Pacific theater as the Army pivots to Asia.

Data to decisions: develop tools and techniques to assimilate, integrate, and process large volumes of heterogeneous data and information from a variety of sources to provide robust situation awareness for decision-making at the operational, tactical, and strategic levels.

Cyber security and operations: conduct research and development to identify and minimize cyber vulnerabilities of Army tactical networks and systems and develop agile tools and networks that can react quickly and operate through cyber attacks.

Protected ground mobility: develop and integrate innovative, 360-degree protection technologies to achieve an order of magnitude weight reduction in ground combat vehicles to provide tactical, operational, and strategic mobility necessary to support national strategic goals in the Pacific theater.

Human performance: conduct research and development to enhance physical and cognitive performance of the Soldier, to include improved resilience, increased socio-cultural awareness, and individual and team training technologies.

Expanded operations in Chemical, Biological, Radiological, Nuclear, and high-yield Explosive (CBRNE) environment: provide the research, development, and engineering efforts to protect our military and nation from the deadly effects of Weapons of Mass Destruction (WMD). This includes capabilities to identify, secure, and eliminate WMD materials; respond to potential WMD events through detection, protection, and decontamination technologies; and establish attribution through forensic analysis of samples taken from the field.

Autonomy-enabled formations: develop and integrate autonomous technologies into ground vehicle formations to unburden Soldiers and empower them to focus on mission-critical tasks and improve tooth-to-tail ratio.

Integrated Soldier protection: develop integrated Soldier protection that combines multiple protection capabilities (e.g., lightweight, breathable, blast and ballistic, fire resistance, extreme environmental, anti-vector, microbial) into one Soldier system.

ENGINEERING LAND COMBAT POWER

RDECOM transitions technologies and capabilities from academia and ARL, through the RDECs, to both programs of record as well as directly to industry. In addition to executing basic, applied, and engineering research, RDECOM also supplies engineers to the PEO community on a reimbursable basis. As systems integrators, RDECOM engineers lead the development of technical specifications and support source selections. In addition, they provide contract technical support, technical oversight of programs, engineering configuration management, hardware and software development, parts obsolescence management, and sustainment engineering support for spare and repair parts. The linkages between RDECOM and our customers provide direct reach back to a robust technology base in ARL and the RDECs with knowledgeable insight into technology development opportunities with commercial partners. This convergence of functions in science and technology, PEO support, and sustainment enables RDECOM to help synchronize the Army's sustainment strategy with technical input for an affordable modernization strategy.

RDECOM provides the systems engineering expertise across a broad range of competencies and engineering disciplines to support all Army PEOs. This expertise uniquely positions RDECOM to integrate systems requirements, technologies, and capabilities to efficiently and effectively generate elegant, low-cost, multi-functional solutions across the materiel enterprise. To deliver on this opportunity, RDECOM is increasing the systems engineering education of our workforce to build an enterprise-level systems engineering capability. RDECOM will refine this capability by establishing a cohort of systems engineers with common training, using enterprise-wide tools to integrate across the PEO community regardless of geographic location. This will allow RDECOM to inform the Army's decisions on future capability investments by developing options within the trade space of technology, performance, risk, and affordability.

To improve the integration process across all aspects of research, development, and engineering, RDECOM will implement a Virtual Laboratory construct. The Virtual Laboratory will allow RDECOM project managers to search, identify, and consult with scientists and engineers from across the enterprise who have the specific skills and experience needed for the project. This will enable RDEC project managers to draw on the core expertise from across the Command to support their specific project without the need to develop a local competency that already exists elsewhere in the Command. The Virtual Laboratory framework will enable the project team to work the requirements, designs, and challenges in a virtual environment, saving time and resources while continuing to build and grow our intellectual capital.

> **Linkages between RDECOM and its customers provide direct reach back to a robust technology base in ARL and RDECs with a direct path through its workforce to the organizations that field and maintain systems.**

RDECOM executes the transition of technologies to PMs and programs of record (including industry) through our extensive and rapid prototyping expertise, with each RDEC performing prototyping specific to its core technical competencies. Prototyping expertise is

ENGINEERING LAND COMBAT POWER (CONT)

critical for the development and transition of new technologies for future systems as well as the efficient sustainment of existing capabilities for legacy systems. The RDEC prototyping capability also involves direct support to the Soldier and Combatant Commands in support of urgent needs and requirements. Prototyping capabilities provide the ability to:

- advance manufacturing technology readiness;

- provide performance and design baselines;

- validate engineering and product data packages;

- inform stakeholders as smart buyers;

- generate intellectual property and government-furnished designs;

- establish and validate manufacturing and production processes (to include temporary and limited production lines);

- provide Better Buying Power;

- define/refine requirements;

- inform Requests For Proposals;

- train the next generation of engineers; and,

- reverse engineer obsolete parts and systems.

RDECOM integrates these assets to provide comprehensive solutions to address near-term needs by developing immediate materiel responses to emerging threats, informing

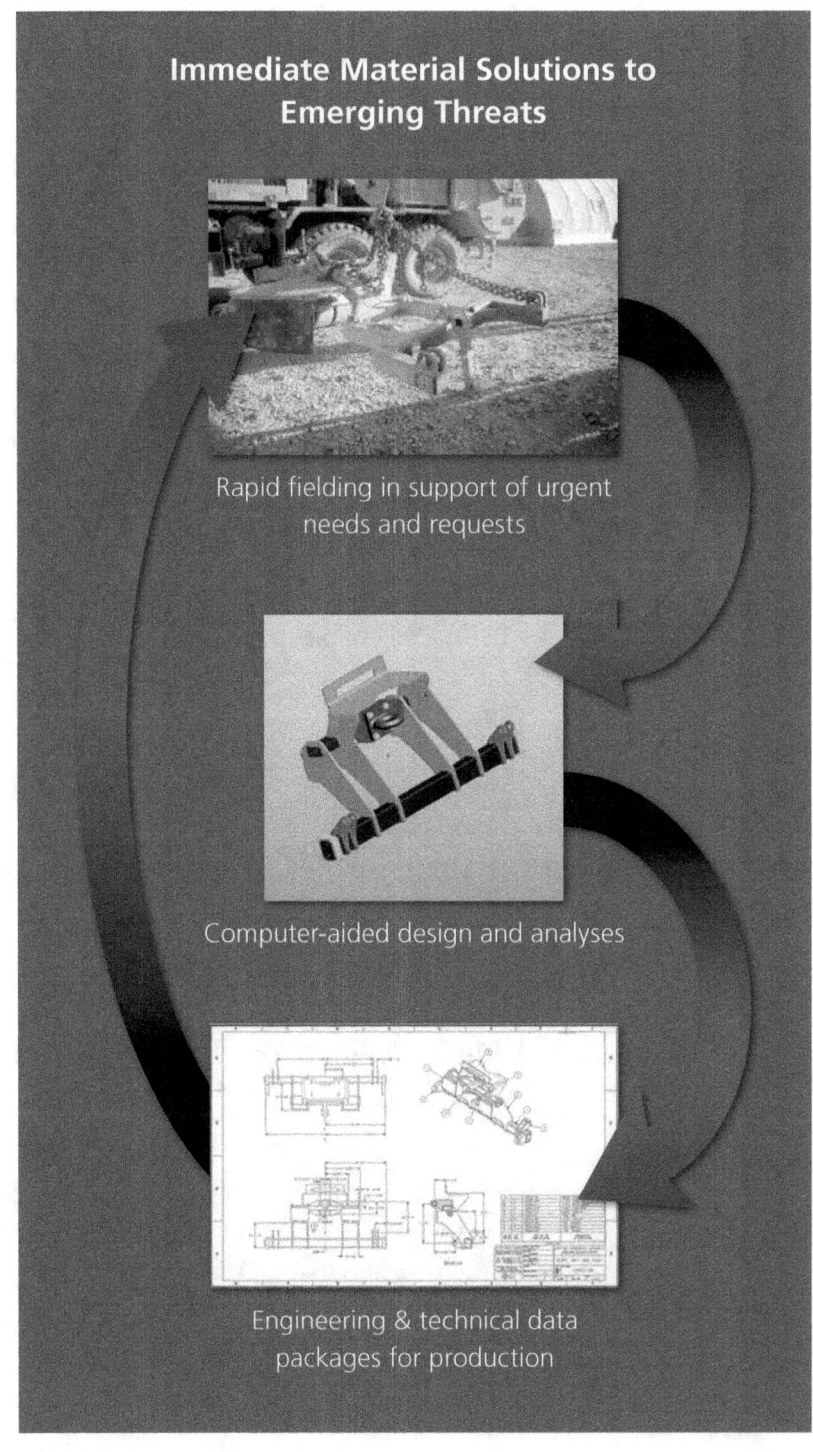

Immediate Material Solutions to Emerging Threats

Rapid fielding in support of urgent needs and requests

Computer-aided design and analyses

Engineering & technical data packages for production

cost-effective investment decisions by providing technology demonstrators, and providing new capabilities to legacy systems.

The Command provides solutions for Army Operational Needs Statements (ONSs), Joint Urgent Operational Needs Statements (JUONSs), and the SOF community through our prototyping capabilities, engineering expertise, and close relationship with the PEOs. These groups often rely on RDECOM's prototyping capabilities and engineering expertise to quickly develop unique systems that are often taken into operational environments shortly after delivery. Using lessons learned and feedback on the performance and employment of those systems, RDECOM engineers, in conjunction with TRADOC, define the development of requirements and drive design of future systems for the Army. Leveraging this knowledge has allowed the Army to make informed decisions regarding requirements, system design, maturity, and performance of new systems.

The integration of engineering matrix support, systems engineering services, and prototyping capabilities across the enterprise uniquely positions RDECOM to be the honest broker to inform Army investment decisions and provide the smart buyer assessment as required by the Weapons Systems Acquisition Reform Act of 2009. RDECOM's highly skilled workforce informs acquisition milestone decisions, assesses the maturity level of technologies, and shapes developmental testing and fielding of materiel. This workforce enables the Army to make informed decisions through unbiased technical expertise that conducts assessments of contract proposals and source selection, assesses technical concepts, conducts system

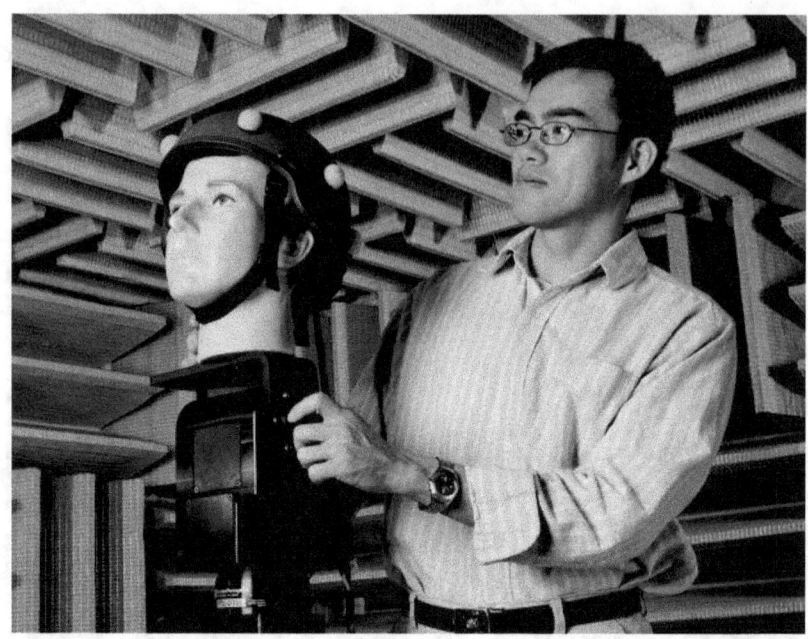

trade-space analysis, evaluates prototypes, and analyzes requirements compliance. These organic skills and missions support Better Buying Power initiatives for Army Acquisition Corps decision makers and are used to support the entire Army's materiel life cycle process, serving as the corporate technical knowledge repository for programs of record.

The current austere fiscal environment has the potential to reduce the number of programs of record that provide new capabilities to the Army. As a result, we may have fewer opportunities to integrate new technologies into existing and future programs of record. To mitigate this risk, RDECOM will serve as the Army's leading science, technology, and engineering

> **RDECOM's core competencies and facilities support every aspect of the Army's materiel life cycle process and serve as the corporate technical knowledge repository for programs of record.**

ENGINEERING LAND COMBAT POWER (CONT)

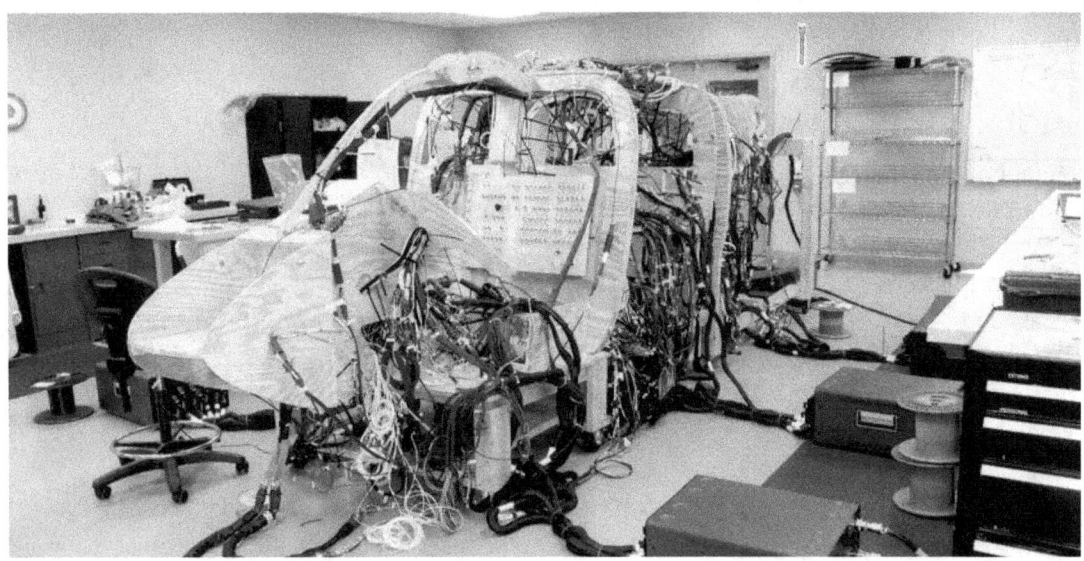

corporate memory by focusing efforts to collect, store, and maintain system data for future use. RDECOM will capture the technical data required to support re-establishment of manufacturing capabilities to address future needs, product upgrades, and modernization in a digital source book. RDECOM's engineering role as product data service provider and our mission to collect, validate, update, and store system product data will grow in importance as procurements are postponed until necessity requires, or available funding enables new investment decisions.

Based on this vision of the future, RDECOM has identified the following areas for increased emphasis in the engineering portfolio:

Enterprise-wide systems engineering: provide rigorous and disciplined processes to deal with multi-dimensional problems, leading to the delivery of integrated solutions using the breadth and depth of the entire RDECOM enterprise within the Virtual Laboratory construct.

Systems analysis and assessments: conduct integrated analyses and assessments in support of requirements, concept designs, human-system integration, vulnerability assessments, and forensics across a broad range of technologies, threats, and operational environments.

Life cycle engineering: provide an integrated cradle-to-grave resource for the development of new systems and life extension of legacy systems.

Prototyping: provide manufacturing technology readiness, performance and design baselines, technical data packages, cost driver identification, reverse engineering capabilities, rapid response to urgent design and manufacturing requirements (to include temporary and limited production lines), and the replacement of obsolete components and subsystems.

DIRECTOR'S INITIATIVES

To execute the AMC Commanding General's priorities, the Director has identified several high-risk, high-payoff initiatives, each designed to provide the Army with a revolutionary new capability. These initiatives are informed by the changing nature of the strategic environment, by TRADOC's highest priority capability gaps, ASA(ALT)'s Top Challenges, and by their potential to provide a leap-ahead capability for the Soldier. Each draws upon a wide range of RDECOM core technical competencies and will require an enterprise approach, thereby serving to focus the efforts of multiple RDECs and ARL on high-priority challenges for the future.

Self-sustaining Forward Operating Base (FOB): Develop a self-sustaining, expeditionary FOB and/or Combat Outpost as an integrated and rapidly deployable system to provide Soldier life-support functions and enable efficient operations. This will be accomplished through the research and development of both materiel and non-materiel solutions and a global engineering architecture whose net result is increased Soldier readiness and improved operational flexibility.

Long-range precision fires: Develop a long-range fires capability that provides affordable precision fires at extended ranges in a GPS-denied environment. This capability will be organic to small units and provide scalable effects on target with minimal collateral damage. This will be accomplished through development of novel energetics and guidance technologies whose net result is timely, adaptive, and increased lethality over a larger area of operations.

Counter Unmanned Aerial Systems (UASs): Develop a capability to detect, identify, and defeat UASs, which potentially represent the next generation of Improvised Explosive Device (IED) threats. This capability will be effective over a wide range of potential threats, from small platforms to larger, more sophisticated platforms. This will be accomplished through the development of sensors, networks, and defeat mechanisms whose net result is increased Soldier survivability.

Robotic team member: Develop a robotic team member with the capability to provide logistics support, situational awareness, and direct and indirect fires for the small unit. This capability will include the ability to operate as a team member with minimal supervision by Soldiers. This will be accomplished through development and integration of novel mobility and manipulation technologies with sensors, fires, human-machine interface, and intelligent-processing technologies whose net result is to extend the situational awareness, survivability, and lethality of the Soldier and small unit.

A UNIQUE NATIONAL ASSET

Today's Army is the most powerful Land Combat Power in the world in part because past technological advances were transformed into revolutionary warfighting capabilities. Virtually every Army system is the result of technologies originally discovered, developed, and demonstrated by the Army's science and technology programs. The Army depends on RDECOM to discover, develop, and demonstrate the high-payoff technologies needed to mitigate emerging threats, provide affordable enhanced capabilities for our legacy systems, and generate revolutionary capabilities designed to make current systems obsolete. Using our technical expertise and understanding of the Soldier, RDECOM bridges the gaps between commercial development and the unique requirements to execute the Army's missions.

RDECOM will mature in our role as the integrating function across the breadth and depth of Army acquisition, to grow in our abilities to eliminate technology blind spots, to bring to bear the rigor and discipline of our systems engineering processes for trade-space analysis in areas where others cannot, and to innovate by looking at a specific problem through a multi-faceted lens focused by the diversity of our expertise. RDECOM's broad research, development, and engineering enterprise, with our extensive prototyping capabilities, provides innovative solutions to mitigate emerging threats and the ability to inform future investments shaped by technology demonstration projects. These initiatives will support critical Army priorities, including AMC's LOE to Enhance Army Capabilities through S&T as well as ASA(ALT)'s ACP 2012 Major Objective to Modernize and Equip the Army to Increase Strategic Depth. RDECOM is informing decisions in the near-term and is poised to inform future affordable modernization strategic decisions by providing both technical and cost data analysis to Army decision authorities.

In addition to our overarching technical breadth and extensive depth, RDECOM is unique in our deep understanding of the Army's mission and military operational environments. RDECOM's relationship and partnership with TRADOC, and extensive experience developing, fielding, and sustaining systems, provides RDECOM with an unmatched understanding of military employment and doctrine. All of these position RDECOM as a unique national asset, defining and operating in the space between the state of the art and the art of the possible, ensuring Army's dominance of Land Combat Power.

REFERENCES

Air Force Science and Technology Strategy 2010

Army Equipment Modernization Strategy, 4 March 2013

Army Materiel Command Strategic Plan 2013–2023 (DRAFT)

Army Posture 2013, 23 April 2012

Army Strategic Planning Guidance, January 2013

Naval S&T Strategic Plan September 2011

Quadrennial Defense Review Report 2010

RDECOM Campaign Plan FY2013–14

TRADOC Memo to AAE, DEC 2012: Science & Technology Investment Areas for Program Objective Memorandum (POM) 15–19

The U.S. Army Capstone Concept, 19 December 2012

U.S. Marine Corps S&T Strategic Plan 2012

ACRONYM LIST

AMC — Army Materiel Command
ARI — Army Research Institute
ARL — Army Research Laboratory
ASA(ALT) — Assistant Secretary of the Army for Acquisition, Logistics and Technology
C4ISR — Command, Control, Communications, Computers, Intelligence, Surveillance, and Reconnaissance
CB — Chemical/Biological
CBRNE — Chemical, Biological, Radiological, Nuclear, and high-yield Explosive
CRADA — Cooperative Research and Development Agreement
CTA — Collaborative Technology Alliance
DARPA — Defense Advanced Research Projects Agency
ERDC — Engineer Research and Development Center
EW — Electronic Warfare
FAST — Field Assistance in Science and Technology
FFRDC — Federally Funded Research and Development Center
FOB — Forward Operating Base
GPS — Global Positioning System
IED — Improvised Explosive Device
ITC — International Technology Center
JUONS — Joint Urgent Operational Needs Statement
LCMC — Life Cycle Management Command
LOE — Line of Effort
MRMC — Medical Research and Materiel Command
MURI — Multidisciplinary University Research Initiative
ONS — Operational Needs Statement
OSD — Office of the Secretary of Defense
PEO — Program Executive Officer
PM — Program Manager
R&D — Research and Development
RDECOM — Research, Development and Engineering Command
RDEC — Research,Development and Engineering Center
RFEC — RDECOM Forward Element Command
SBIR — Small Business Innovative Research
S&T — Science and Technology
SMDC — Space and Missile Defense Command
SOF — Special Operation Forces
TBI — Traumatic Brain Injury
TRADOC — Training and Doctrine Command
UARC — University Affiliated Research Center
UAS — Unmanned Aerial System
WMD — Weapon of Mass Destruction

APPENDIX A: RDECOM ORGANIZATIONAL STRUCTURE

APPENDIX A: RDECOM ORGANIZATIONAL STRUCTURE (CONT)

AVIATION AND MISSILE RESEARCH, DEVELOPMENT AND ENGINEERING CENTER (AMRDEC)

Director
Mr. Eric Edwards

MISSION:
Deliver collaborative and innovative technical capabilities for responsive and cost-effective research, product development, and life cycle systems engineering solutions.

OVERVIEW:
AMRDEC is the Army's focal point for providing research, development, and engineering technology and services for aviation and missile platforms across the life cycle. AMRDEC provides a wide array of technologies, hardware and software applications, and products and services. These run the gamut from game-changing technologies to detect and destroy threats, enhance performance, lethality, survivability, and reliability of aviation and missile systems along with programs to miniaturize missile and aircraft components, provide modeling and simulation applications for these technologies and systems, and the associated training applications. Also, AMRDEC serves as the Department of Defense (DoD) lead for rotorcraft Science and Technology (S&T) as well as gel propellants. In addition, AMRDEC has one of the few Capability Maturity Model (CMM) Level 4 software engineering facilities in the Army, certified by the world-renowned Software Engineering Institute (SEI). The enormous capability provided by the AMRDEC Prototype Integration Facility (PIF) has quickly become the Army's premier rapid response organization. These capabilities give a sense of the breadth of end-to-end capability that AMRDEC provides to its customers.

PEOPLE:
- 3,140 civilians
  - 2,504 scientists and engineers
    - 102 doctorates
    - 806 master's degrees
    - 1,578 bachelor's degrees
- 22 military
- 6,326 contractors

SAMPLE OF UNIQUE FACILITIES

Advanced Prototype Experimentation

National Full-Scale Aerodynamics Complex

ARMAMENT RESEARCH, DEVELOPMENT AND ENGINEERING CENTER (ARDEC)

Director
Dr. Gerardo
J. Melendez

MISSION:
Empower, unburden, and protect the Soldier by providing superior armaments solutions that dominate the battlefield.

OVERVIEW:
ARDEC develops advanced weapons, ammunition, and fire control systems for the U.S. Army, providing the technology for more than 90 percent of the Army's lethality. These technologies include energetics, warheads, directed energy, integrated weapon systems, and networked fire control. ARDEC understands the importance of working with Soldiers to provide solutions to their unique challenges and equipment requirements. This is reflected by ARDEC's achievement in winning 34 out of 100 Army's Greatest Inventions awards, as judged by Soldiers, since 2002.

ARDEC has validated its best value status by external assessment in national and international organizational competition. ARDEC is the only Department of Defense (DoD) organization to become the Baldrige recipient and one of the few in the world that has garnered Baldrige and Shingo recognition. ARDEC is also proud to be the sole U.S. government organization to currently hold the Capability Maturity Model Integration (CMMI) for Development maturity level 5 distinction at its Armament Software Engineering Center.

PEOPLE:
- 3,718 civilians
    - 2,767 scientists and engineers
        - 62 doctorates
        - 846 master's degrees
        - 1,853 bachelor's degrees
- 22 military
- 623 contractors

SAMPLE OF UNIQUE FACILITIES	Remote Weapon Station Software Engineering Facility	Soft Recovery System Facility (Scat Gun)

APPENDIX A: RDECOM ORGANIZATIONAL STRUCTURE (CONT)

ARMY RESEARCH LABORATORY (ARL)

Director
Dr. Thomas Russell

MISSION:
Provide innovative science, technology, and analyses to enable full spectrum operations.

OVERVIEW:
The Soldiers of today and tomorrow depend on the Army's corporate laboratory to deliver the scientific discoveries, technological advances, and the analyses that provide Soldiers with the capabilities with which to execute full-spectrum operations.

ARL's investment portfolio is focused on discovery, innovation, and technology transition principally to the Research, Development, and Engineering Centers (RDECs), but also to our other partners in the Army Transformation Program Executive Offices/Program Managers (PEOs/PMs), the Army Test and Evaluation Command (ATEC), the Training and Doctrine Command (TRADOC) Battle Labs, the other services, and the private sector.

PEOPLE:
- 1,975 civilians
  - 1,379 scientists and engineers
    - 552 doctorates
    - 479 master's degrees
    - 348 bachelor's degrees
- 37 military
- 914 contractors

SAMPLE OF UNIQUE FACILITIES

Environment for Auditory Research

DoD Supercomputing Resource Center

COMMUNICATIONS–ELECTRONICS RESEARCH, DEVELOPMENT AND ENGINEERING CENTER (CERDEC)

Director
Ms. Jill Smith

MISSION:
To develop and integrate Command, Control, Communications, Computers, Intelligence, Surveillance, and Reconnaissance (C4ISR) technologies that enable information and cyber dominance, and decisive lethality for the networked Soldier.

OVERVIEW:
Whether Soldier-borne or integrated onto ground or aviation platforms, the Army relies on CERDEC's technical expertise to develop, seek out, and engineer C4ISR integrated capabilities to address Soldier needs.

CERDEC's government-unique and world-unique facilities support a broad range of technical areas that leverage expertise in the radio, digital, and electronic realms of information technology and systems engineering.

PEOPLE:
* 2,108 civilians
  - 1,620 scientists and engineers
    - 105 doctorates
    - 941 master's degrees
    - 515 bachelor's degrees
* 42 military
* 1,044 contractors

SAMPLE OF UNIQUE FACILITIES	Soldier Radio Waveform Reference Implementation Lab (SRW RIL)	Antennas and Spectrum Analysis Lab

APPENDIX A: RDECOM ORGANIZATIONAL STRUCTURE (CONT)

EDGEWOOD CHEMICAL BIOLOGICAL CENTER (ECBC)

Director
Mr. Joseph Wienand

MISSION:
Integrate life cycle science, engineering, and operation solutions to counter chemical, biological, radiological, nuclear, and high-yield explosive (CBRNE) threats to U.S. forces and the nation.

OVERVIEW:
As the nation's principal research and development laboratory for countering chemical and biological weapons of mass destruction, ECBC provides solutions to complex CBRNE threats for both the military and the nation. Products, scientific advances, and critical advice are provided to support the total military acquisition life cycle from basic and applied research through demilitarization to address our nation's unique needs. ECBC leverages a talented workforce with specialized experience as well as state-of-the-art CBRNE equipment and facilities. Utilizing these intrinsic capabilities, ECBC can safely design, build, test, and support projects from original conception to a final product completely in-house.

With a long history of developing cutting-edge technologies in the areas of detection, protection, and decontamination, ECBC is considered a national resource for CBRNE solutions. ECBC will continue to sustain the core competencies and workforce to counter enduring and emerging chemical and biological threats and continue to create success for Soldier and CBRNE clients to meet the evolving CBRNE defense needs.

PEOPLE:
- 1,198 civilians
    - 674 scientists and engineers
        - 95 doctorates
        - 179 master's degrees
        - 396 bachelor's degrees
- 0 military
- 331 contractors

SAMPLE OF UNIQUE FACILITIES

Chemical Transfer Facility (CTF)

Sample Receipt Facility (SRF)

NATICK SOLDIER RESEARCH, DEVELOPMENT AND ENGINEERING CENTER (NSRDEC)

Director
Dr. John Obusek

MISSION:
RD&E to maximize the Soldier's survivability, sustainability, mobility, combat effectiveness, and field quality of life by treating the Soldier as a system.

OVERVIEW:
NSRDEC supports the current fight and transforms the future force with the Soldier as the decisive edge.

With a unique human-centric focus, NSRDEC adds value through basic science; technology generation, application, and transition enabling rapid fielding of the right equipment; Soldier systems technology integration and transition; and solving field problems rapidly.

NSRDEC's vision is to be the leader in empowering the world's most capable Soldiers.

PEOPLE:
- 695 civilians
  - 340 scientists and engineers
    - 53 doctorates
    - 162 master's degrees
    - 313 bachelor's degrees
- 25 military
- 76 contractors

SAMPLE OF UNIQUE FACILITIES

Doriot Climactic Chambers

Center for Military Biomechanics Research

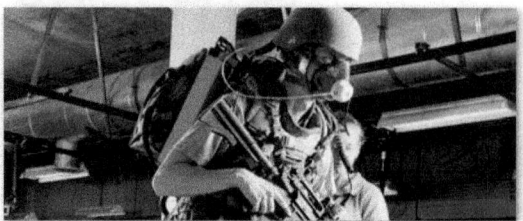

APPENDIX A: RDECOM ORGANIZATIONAL STRUCTURE (CONT)

TANK AUTOMOTIVE RESEARCH, DEVELOPMENT AND ENGINEERING CENTER (TARDEC)

Director
Dr. Paul Rogers

MISSION:
Develop, integrate, and sustain the right technology solutions for all manned and unmanned Department of Defense (DoD) ground vehicle systems and combat service support equipment to improve current force effectiveness and provide superior capabilities for the future force.

OVERVIEW:
TARDEC is the nation's laboratory for developing advanced military ground vehicle technologies, process integration expertise, and system-of-systems engineering solutions for force projection technology, ground vehicle power and mobility, ground vehicle robotics, ground systems survivability, and vehicle electronics and architecture.

PEOPLE:
- 1,419 civilians
  - 1,086 scientists and engineers
    - 43 doctorates
    - 465 master's degrees
    - 439 bachelor's degrees
- 11 military
- 221 contractors

SAMPLE OF UNIQUE FACILITIES	Ground Systems Power and Energy Laboratory	Ride Motion Simulator/Ground Vehicle Simulation Laboratory

APPENDIX B: ARMY CHALLENGES AND INVESTMENT PRIORITIES

ASA(ALT) ARMY TOP CHALLENGES

1. Greater force protection (Soldier, vehicle, base) to ensure survivability across all operations

2. Ease overburdened Soldiers in small units

3. Deliver timely mission command and tactical intelligence to provide situational awareness in all environments

4. Reduce expense of storing, transporting, and waste handling of consumables

5. Create operational overmatch (enhanced lethality and accuracy)

6. Achieve operational maneuverability in all environments and at high operational tempo

7. Enable ability to operate in CBRNE environment

8. Improve early detection of Traumatic Brain Injury (TBI)

9. Improve operational energy

10. Improve individual and team training

11. Reduce life cycle cost of future Army capabilities

APPENDIX B: ARMY CHALLENGES AND INVESTMENT PRIORITIES (CONT)

TRADOC SCIENCE AND TECHNOLOGY INVESTMENT AREAS

1. Countering Weapons of Mass Destruction (WMDs) and proliferation at a large scale

2. Extended range precision surface to air and surface to surface fires

3. Army's role in assured access to global commons

4. Deliver timely mission command and tactical intelligence to provide situational awareness and communications in all environments and eliminate tactical surprise

5. Improve early detection of TBI

6. Improve operational energy to reduce demand and improve tooth-to-tail ratio

7. Improve individual and team training

8. Greater force protection (Soldier, vehicle, base) to ensure survivability across all operations

9. Achieve operational maneuverability in all environments and at high operational tempo with improved survivability

10. Create operational overmatch (enhanced lethality and accuracy)

11. Enable ability to operate in CBRNE environments

12. Ease overburdened Soldiers in small units without reducing operational effectiveness

13. Reduce life cycle cost of future Army capabilities

14. Reduce expense of storing, transporting, and waste handling of consumables

APPENDIX C: EXPANDED CORE TECHNICAL COMPETENCIES

Fundamental Research
- Materials Sciences
- Information Sciences
- Ballistics
- Aeromechanics
- Human Performance

Aviation Systems Technologies
- Aerodynamics/Aeromechanics (Structures, Flight Control, Crew Station, Survivability)
- Weapons and Sensor Integration (Avionics)
- Propulsion
- Aviation Autonomy and Teaming (Manned and Unmanned)

Weapons and Munitions Technologies
- Warhead/Lethal Mechanisms and Fuzing (Energetics, Guidance/Navigation/Control)
- Countermine/IED Neutralization
- Directed Energy/Non-Lethal
- Fire Control

Chemical and Biological (CB) Technologies
- CB Warfare (Aerosol Physics, Inhalation Toxicology, Filtration Science, CB Testing)
- CB Spectroscopy/Algorithms
- Chemical Munitions (CB Agent Handling/ Surety/Demilitarization)
- Smoke and Obscurants

Ground Systems Technologies
- Ground System Design (Propulsion, Mobility, Survivability, Structures)
- Robotics
- Alternative Fuels and Lubricants
- Weapon and Sensor Integration (Vehicle Electronics and Power Management)

Communications and Electronics Technologies
- Space and Terrestrial Communications (Spectrum Management)
- Sensors (Position, Navigation, and Timing, EO/IR, Counter IED, Radar)
- Mission Command
- Cyber/Electronic Warfare (EW)
- Power Generation and Storage

Missile/Rocket Technologies
- Structures (Propulsion, Energetics, Lethal Mechanisms, Flight Control)
- Guidance/Navigation (Embedded Electronics and Computers, Infrared Sensor/Seekers)

Soldier Technologies
- Protection Materials (Individual, Collective, Shelter Systems)
- Physical/Physiological/Cognitive Performance (Behavior Research/ Embedded Cognition, Collective Performance/Teaming)
- Biological Anthropology/Mechanics
- Combat Feeding/Food Science

Cross Command Engineering Specialties
- Systems Engineering (Anthropo-centric Systems Engineering, Systems Integration)
- System/Subsystem Concept Design and Assessment
- Software Engineering
- Reliability Engineering
- Sustainment Engineering/Industrial Base Analysis/Obsolescence Management
- Prototyping, Modeling/Simulation
- Quality Engineering and Management
- System Safety
- Human Factors Engineering

APPENDIX C: EXPANDED CORE TECHNICAL COMPETENCIES (CONT)

Cross Command Engineering Specialties (cont)

- Manufacturing/Production Support (Product/Technical Data)
- Survivability, Lethality, Vulnerability Analysis and Assessment

www.ingramcontent.com/pod-product-compliance
Lightning Source LLC
Chambersburg PA
CBHW052024280526
45793CB00005B/1116

* 9 7 8 1 5 0 5 3 9 6 0 9 6 *